FLOATING and DISAPPEARING

✻ M A G I C *✻*

to

ENCHANT and EXCITE

Jessica Rusick

Super Sandcastle

An Imprint of Abdo Publishing
abdobooks.com

abdobooks.com

Printed in the United States of America, North Mankato, Minnesota
102019
012020

THIS BOOK CONTAINS RECYCLED MATERIALS

Design: Aruna Rangarajan, Mighty Media, Inc.
Production: Mighty Media, Inc.
Editor: Rachael Thomas
Design Elements: Shutterstock Images
Cover Photograph: Mighty Media, Inc., Shutterstock Images
Interior Photographs: carebott/iStockphoto, p. 7; John Sommer/iStockphoto, p. 12 (kid); Mighty Media, Inc., pp. 5, 8, 9, 10, 11, 12, 13, 14, 15, 16, 17, 18, 19, 20, 21, 22, 23, 24, 26, 27, 28, 29, 30, 31; Shutterstock Images, pp. 6, 8 (dinner roll), 9 (salt, spoon), 11 (kid), 21 (kid), 24 (street performer), 28 (kid), 30 (group of kids), 31 (bottom); Wikimedia Commons, pp. 4, 25
The following manufacturers/names appearing in this book are trademarks: Aleene's®
Original Tacky Glue®, Heinz®, Pyrex®, Scotch®, Soap Expressions™, Styrofoam™

Library of Congress Control Number: 2019943205

Publisher's Cataloging-in-Publication Data
Names: Rusick, Jessica, author.
Title: Floating and disappearing magic to enchant and excite / by Jessica Rusick
Description: Minneapolis, Minnesota : Abdo Publishing, 2020 | Series: Super simple magic and illusions
Identifiers: ISBN 9781532191589 (lib. bdg.) | ISBN 9781532178313 (ebook)
Subjects: LCSH: Magic tricks--Juvenile literature. | Sleight of hand--Juvenile literature. | Optical illusions--Juvenile literature. | Science and magic--Juvenile literature.
Classification: DDC 793.8--dc23

Super SandCastle™ books are created by a team of professional educators, reading specialists, and content developers around five essential components—phonemic awareness, phonics, vocabulary, text comprehension, and fluency—to assist young readers as they develop reading skills and strategies and increase their general knowledge. All books are written, reviewed, and leveled for guided reading and early reading intervention programs for use in shared, guided, and independent reading and writing activities to support a balanced approach to literacy instruction.

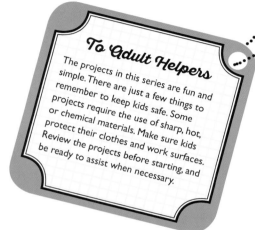

To Adult Helpers
The projects in this series are fun and simple. There are just a few things to remember to keep kids safe. Some projects require the use of sharp, hot, or chemical materials. Make sure kids protect their clothes and work surfaces. Review the projects before starting, and be ready to assist when necessary.

Contents

THE MAGIC OF
Floating and Disappearing

Have you ever seen a person float above the ground? Or an everyday object that doesn't stick around? These are floating and disappearing tricks!

Floating and disappearing tricks seem to **defy** the laws of nature. But like all magic tricks, there are **techniques** behind each **illusion**.

In 1918, magician Harry Houdini made an elephant vanish!

FLOATING AND DISAPPEARING
Tips and Techniques

Floating and disappearing tricks take preparation to pull off. Some **rely** on hidden **props**, quick movements, or **sleight of hand**.

Some floating and disappearing tricks also depend on carefully planned angles. Angles allow you to control what the **audience** sees. Performing a trick at the right angle can hide secret props and movements.

How well a trick works might depend on how quickly you can perform a certain movement. One wrong move can make or break a floating and disappearing trick!

1 Read the steps carefully.

2 Practice in front of a friend to figure out the best angle for a trick.

3 Come up with jokes and stories to **distract** your audience.

Remember, the brain is smart! Tricking it takes precision.

PRACTICE AND PRESENTATION

Even if you've spent lots of time on a trick, it might not work out. That's okay! Like all magic tricks, floating and disappearing tricks take practice to get right. If you didn't fool an **audience**, try again.

The way you **present** your tricks matters. Don't let your audience see you set up or any secret **props**. If a trick must be viewed from a certain distance or angle, don't let your audience see it any other way!

FLOATING AND DISAPPEARING MAGIC

Tool Kit

Here are some of the materials that you will need for the tricks in this book.

CLEAR PLASTIC SHEETS

CLEAR TAPE

CLOTH

DINNER ROLL

DRINKING STRAWS

FUNNEL

DRINKING GLASSES

FORK

GLASS BOTTLES

SALT

GLUE

GLYCERIN

KETCHUP PACKETS

PLASTIC WATER BOTTLE

PLAYING CARD

SCISSORS

RULER

SPOON

STYROFOAM CUP

TOOTHPICKS

VANISHING TOOTHPICK

Make a toothpick disappear
from your hand!

Materials

+ toothpick
+ clear tape

1 To prepare the trick, tape the tip of the toothpick to your thumbnail. The toothpick should lay on top of your thumb.

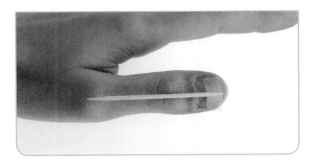

2 Stand in front of your **audience**. Make a fist so your fingers cover the tip of your thumb and hide the tape.

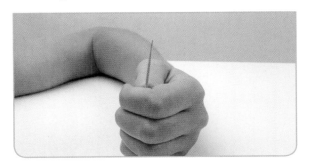

3 Quickly open your hand and turn it palm up. It will look like the toothpick is gone! It is really on the back of your thumb.

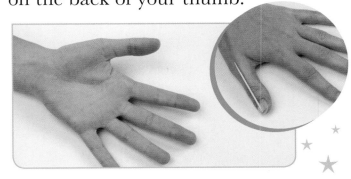

4 Slip your hand into your pocket. Remove the toothpick from your thumb while your hand is hidden.

Amazing

11

DISAPPEARING BOTTLE

Make a bottle disappear from sight!

Materials
+ 2 small, empty glass bottles
+ water
+ glycerin
+ 2 clear drinking glasses
+ funnel (optional)
+ drinking straw (optional)

1 Fill one glass bottle with water and the other with glycerin. If necessary, use a funnel or straw to pour.

2 Fill one drinking glass two-thirds full of water. Fill the other two-thirds full of glycerin.

3 Place the bottle of water in the glass of water. Ask your **audience** if they can see the bottle through the glass.

4 Now place the bottle of glycerin in the glass of glycerin. Where did the bottle go?

BEHIND THE MAGIC

Light travels through water and glass at different speeds. This change in speed causes light to **refract**. Our eyes see this refraction, so we see the water bottle. Light travels through glycerin and glass at the same speed. So, light does not refract, and we do not see the bottle.

INVISIBLE STRAW

Make a straw vanish and reappear before your audience's eyes!

Materials

+ drinking straw

1 Hold the ends of a straw between your thumb, index, and middle fingers.

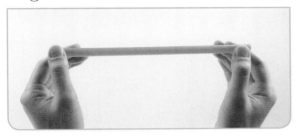

2 Push on the right end of the straw with your fingers.

3 As you push, quickly release the thumb of your left hand. Keep your hand as still as possible.

4 The straw should snap to the inside of your arm, where your **audience** cannot see it.

5 Make the straw reappear! Grab the middle of the straw with your left hand. Extend your right fingers and slide the straw back into view.

PROP SWAP

After you can make a straw vanish, try the trick with a pen! Because it is stiffer than a straw, it will be slightly harder to snap back. However, a pen will be easier to hide! What else can you make disappear?

FLOATING CUP

Make a cup float
in your hands!

Materials
+ Styrofoam cup

1 Use your thumb to make a hole in the side of a Styrofoam cup. Your thumb should fit tightly in the hole.

2 Place the cup in front of an **audience**. Make sure the audience can't see the hole.

3 Wrap both hands around the cup. While you do this, slip one thumb into the secret hole.

4 Raise the cup and slowly move your fingers away. It will look like the cup is floating between your hands!

wow!

BOBBING KETCHUP

Make a ketchup packet float and fall on command!

Materials

+ plastic water bottle without label
+ water
+ ketchup packet
+ salt (optional)
+ funnel (optional)
+ spoon (optional)

1 Put the ketchup packet in the bottle. Fill the bottle with water.

2 If the packet does not float, add a tablespoon of salt to the water. Close the bottle. Shake it until the salt **dissolves**. Repeat this step until the packet floats.

3 Lightly squeeze the water bottle. The ketchup packet should sink when you squeeze the bottle and float when you let go. You can even get it to stop in the middle!

4 Practice making the ketchup packet rise and fall. Then, show your floating ketchup to an **audience**!

BUOYANT BUN

Materials
+ cloth
+ fork
+ dinner roll

Make your dinner hover!

1 Hold up a cloth. Hide a fork behind the cloth in one hand.

2 Drape the cloth over the dinner roll. As you do this, stick the fork in the roll.

3 Ask a **volunteer** to **chant** a magic word or wave their hands over the cloth.

4 Grab both sides of the cloth, while still gripping the hidden fork in one hand. Lift both hands. Make sure the roll stays under the cloth. It will look like the roll is floating!

Whoa!

MAGIC LEVITATION

Make yourself hover above the ground!

Materials

+ large, open space with no shiny surfaces

1 Stand eight to ten feet (2 to 3 m) from your **audience**. Position your body at a 45-degree angle from the audience. The audience should be able to see one of your feet and your other foot's heel.

2 Place your feet about ¾ inch (2 cm) apart. Make sure they line up with each other.

3 **Distract** the audience with a story about how you learned to float. While you are talking, shift your weight to the foot that is mostly hidden.

4 Raise your arms as if you are beginning to float. This will continue to distract your audience.

5 Raise your front foot about one inch (2.5 cm) off the ground. Be careful not to raise it too high, or the audience will see your hidden foot.

CONTINUED ON NEXT PAGE

6 Rise up on the ball of your hidden foot slightly. Raise your front foot alongside it. Keep your heels even.

7 Hold the pose for five seconds, then let your feet come down. As you lower your feet, lower your arms as well. You just **levitated**!

A street performer seems to levitate with no support.

Iconic Illusionist

David Copperfield is an **illusionist** famous for his large-scale performances. In 1983, he made the Statue of Liberty disappear in front of a live **audience**!

First, Copperfield raised a curtain to block the audience's view of the statue. Then, a secret platform under the audience slowly rotated away from the statue. When the curtain dropped, the audience saw an empty space! This was because they no longer faced the statue.

LEVITATING CARD

Make a card float in the palm of your hand!

Materials

+ clear plastic sheet
+ scissors
+ ruler
+ playing card
+ glue

1 Cut a strip of plastic that is ¾ inches (2 cm) wide.

2 Trim the strip to be the same length as the playing card.

3 Place a dot of glue in the center of the back of the playing card.

4 Set the plastic on the glue so it is centered lengthwise on the card. Let the glue dry.

CONTINUED ON NEXT PAGE

5 Once the glue is dry, you should be able to bend both ends of the plastic toward you. The special card you made is called a **gimmick** card.

6 Show the gimmick card to the **audience**. Make sure the audience cannot see the back of the card.

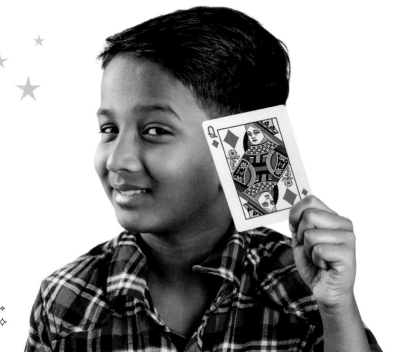

7 Place the card in your palm. Hold one end of the plastic strip between your ring and pinky fingers. Hold the other end of the plastic between your thumb and index finger.

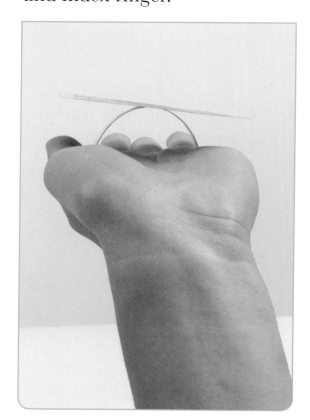

8 Slowly squeeze your hand. Keep your thumb as straight as possible while you squeeze. The card will appear to float above your palm!

9 Slowly relax your hand to bring the card back down.

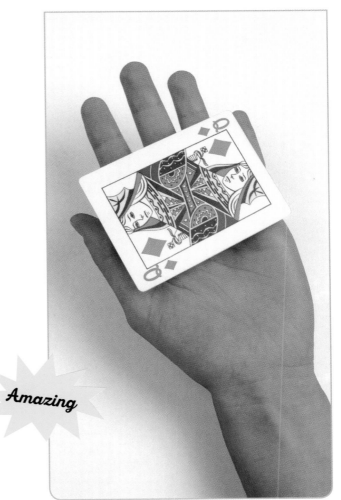

Amazing

HOST A
MAGIC SHOW!

Magic tricks need more than **props** and practice. They also require an **audience**! When you have a few tricks ready, put on a magic show for your friends and family. You could try setting up a stage for it. Or, keep it simple and gather your audience around a table.

Whoa

Cool

TIPS TO BECOME A
Master Magician

Be **confident** when **presenting** your magic tricks.

Use stories and other **distractions** to make your performances stand out.

Keep each trick's secrets to yourself. A little mystery makes magic fun!

Glossary of Magic Words

audience – a group of people watching a performance.

chant – a short, simple set of words or sounds sung on just a note or two.

confident – feeling sure you can do something.

defy – to challenge or resist something.

dissolve – to become part of a liquid.

distract – to cause to turn away from one's original focus of interest. A distraction is something that distracts.

gimmick – a trick or device used to fool somebody.

illusion – something that looks real but is not. Somebody who practices illusions is an illusionist.

levitate – to rise or float up into the air.

precision – the quality or state of being accurate or exact.

present – to show or talk about something to a group or the public. A performance is called a presentation.

prop – an object that is carried or used by an actor in a performance.

refract – to cause a ray, such as light, to bend when it passes at an angle from one medium into another, such as from air into water.

rely – to depend on.

sleight of hand – a hand movement that tricks people.

techniques – a method or style in which something is done.

volunteer – a person who offers to do something.